Psalm 23

The Lord is my shepherd, I shall
not want.
He makes me lie down in green
pastures;
he leads me beside still waters;
he restores my soul.
He leads me in right paths
for his name's sake.

... Surely goodness and mercy shall
follow me
all the days of my life,
and I shall dwell in the house
of the Lord
my whole life long

PRECIOUS MOMENTS

To

George Fredrick Cade

Love

From

The Shanley's

Date

May 19, 2002

Caring Angels

The Helen Steiner Rice Foundation

Whatever the celebration, whatever the day, whatever the event, whatever the occasion, Helen Steiner Rice possessed the ability to express the appropriate feeling for that particular moment in time.

A happening became happier, a sentiment more sentimental, a memory more memorable because of her deep sensitivity to put into understandable language the emotion being experienced. Her positive attitude, her concern for others, and her love of God are identifiable threads woven into her life, her works...and even her death.

Prior to her passing, she established the Helen Steiner Rice Foundation, a nonprofit corporation whose purpose is to award grants to worthy charitable programs and aid the elderly, the needy, and the poor. In her lifetime, these were the individuals about whom Mrs. Rice was greatly concerned.

Royalties from the sale of this book will add to the financial capabilities of the Helen Steiner Rice Foundation. Each year this foundation presents grants to various qualified, worthwhile, and charitable programs. Because of her foresight, her caring, and her deep convictions, Helen Steiner Rice continues to touch a countless number of lives. Thank you for your assistance in helping to keep Helen's dream alive.

Virginia J. Ruehlmann, Administrator
The Helen Steiner Rice Foundation
Suite 2100, Atrium Two
221 East Fourth Street
Cincinnati, Ohio 45202

PRECIOUS MOMENTS

Caring Angels

Verses by Helen Steiner Rice

Compiled by Virginia J. Ruehlmann

Illustrations by Samuel J. Butcher

Fleming H. Revell
A Division of Baker Book House Co
Grand Rapids, Michigan 49516

Published by Fleming H. Revell,
a division of Baker Book House
P.O. Box 6287, Grand Rapids, Michigan 49516-6287
All rights reserved.

Sixth printing, October 1998

Printed in the United States of America.

For current information about all releases from
Baker Book House, visit our web site:
http://www.bakerbooks.com/

Library of Congress Cataloging-in-Publication Data

Rice, Helen Steiner.
    Precious moments : caring angels / verses by Helen Steiner Rice ;
compiled by Virginia J. Ruehlmann ; illustrations by Samuel J. Butcher.
        p.   cm.
    ISBN 0-8007-7139-7
    1. Angels--Poetry. I. Ruehlmann, Virginia J. II. Butcher, Samuel J.
(Samuel John), 1939–   . III. Title. IV. Title:
PS3568.I28P73   1994
811'.54 – dc20   94–17006

Contents

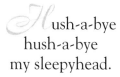
ush-a-bye
hush-a-bye
my sleepyhead.

Angels are waiting
to tuck you in bed.

9

*G*o to sleep
go to sleep
close your bright eyes.
Nighttime is tumbling
out of the skies.

$\mathcal{A}$ngels are waiting
their vigil to keep.
The sandman is filling
your wee eyes with sleep.

*H*ush-a-bye
hush-a-bye
hush-a-bye, sweet.
Playtime is over
for tired, tiny feet.

Close your eyes, honey,
sleepytime's here.
Good night,
little darling.
Good night,
little dear.

While angels
dwell in Christmas skies,
we must come to realize
that all year through.

in many places
we catch a glimpse
of angel faces.

Still streams melting
in the spring,
rippling over
rocks that sing;

*B*arren, windswept,
lonely hills turning gold
with daffodils

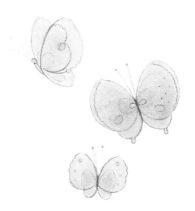

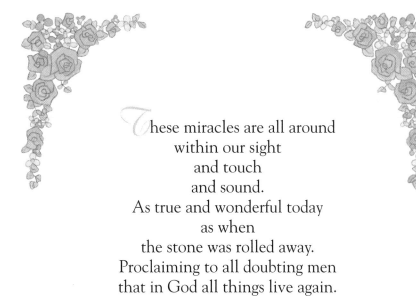

These miracles are all around
within our sight
and touch
and sound.
As true and wonderful today
as when
the stone was rolled away.
Proclaiming to all doubting men
that in God all things live again.

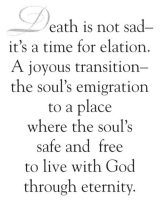

$\mathcal{D}$eath is not sad–
it's a time for elation.
A joyous transition–
the soul's emigration
to a place
where the soul's
safe and free
to live with God
through eternity.

*P*rayers for big
and
little
things

fly
heavenward
on angels'
wings.

$\mathcal{H}$e who walked by Galilee,
touched the blind
and made them see,
cured the man
who long was lame
when he but called
God's holy name,

$\mathcal{W}$ill keep you
safely in his care,
and when you need him,
he'll be there.

We, like flowers
too must sleep
until we're called

to live in that place
where angels sing
and where there is
eternal spring.

$\mathcal{O}$n life's busy
thoroughfares
we meet angels
unawares,

43

But we are too busy
to listen or hear...
too busy to stop
and recognize
the grief that lies
in another's eyes.

Too busy to offer
to help or to share,
too busy to sympathize
or care.
Too busy to do
the good things we should.
Telling ourselves
we would
if we could.

*N*ature's great forces
are found in quiet things
like softly falling snowflakes
drifting down on angels' wings.

*O*r petals
dropping soundlessly
from a lovely
full-blown rose...

$\mathcal{S}$o God
comes closest to us
when our souls
are in repose.

I remember so well
the prayer I said
each night
as my mother
tucked me
in bed.

Today this same prayer
is still the best way
to sign off with God
at the end of the day.

Ask him
your soul to safely keep
as you wearily close
your tired eyes
in sleep.

*F*eeling content
that the Father above
will hold you secure
in his strong arms
of love.

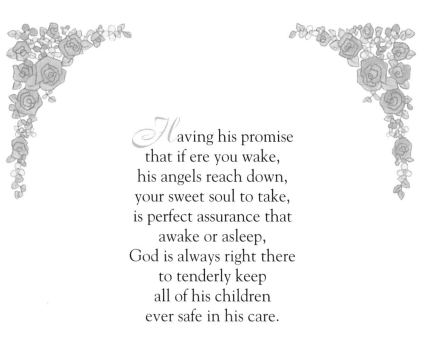

Having his promise
that if ere you wake,
his angels reach down,
your sweet soul to take,
is perfect assurance that
awake or asleep,
God is always right there
to tenderly keep
all of his children
ever safe in his care.

So
into his hands
each night
as I sleep,
I commend
my soul
to the dear Lord
to keep.
Knowing that if
my soul
should take flight,
it will soar
to the land
where there is
no night.